For my mother
and
in memory of my father

Ingrid de Kok

Familiar Ground

Ravan Press Johannesburg

Published by Ravan Press (Pty) Ltd,
P O Box 31134, Braamfontein 2017
Johannesburg, South Africa

First published 1988
Second impression 1991

Printed and bound by Sigma Press (Pty) Ltd, Pretoria

ISBN 0 86975 326 6

Cover photograph: David Goldblatt

Acknowledgements are due to the following journals, in which some of these poems first appeared under the name Ingrid Fiske

Canada and the United States

Descant, Brick, The Fiddlehead, event, Room of One's Own, TriQuarterly

South Africa

Sesame, Contrast, UpStream, Stir, Izwi, Staffrider

Acknowledgement is also due to the anthology, *LIP,* in which *Leavetaking* and *Sun, Aloe, Rain* first appeared.

I would like to thank Mary Anne Bähr for her considerable assistance in the preparation of this book and Cyril Couve for his support and encouragement.

Contents

1 In a Hot Country

To drink its water

1
Home is where the heart is:
a tin can tied to a stray dog.

The only truth is home truth:
preserves on the winter shelf.

Those who carry their homes on their backs
live for hundreds of years,
moving inch by inch from birth to lagoon.

2
Beside the beaten path
to the veld where I once played,
dry riverbed and unwashed clothes
grey lizards on the rocks.
My shadow squats in the shade of a thorn
where children sift and store
the remnants of corroded bins.
Over the path, the rocks, the tree,
marauding sky, fiercer than memory.

3
In a hot country
light is a leper,
water the eye of a goat
on the fork of an honoured guest.

The tap in the camp drips onto the bone of the gum.

And those in the cool green houses,

owners of the sweet white water,
owners of the bins and wells,
die swollen, host and guest of a herd of eyes
washing within them.

4

To return home, you have to drink its water,
in a drought, you have to drink its water,
even from the courtyard well,
the water blossoming in the gut,
or brackish, from a burning trough,
flypaper on your tongue,
pooling your hands,
bending when you drink.

5

Home is where the heart is:
husk of heat on the back.

The sky enters into the skin,
the sky's red ants
crawl over the shoulders.

This bending body is my only body.
I bend and drink
the shadow in the water.

Sun, Aloe, Rain

1

On the edge of scrub, where I grew up,
there were many veld fires in the brittle summer
and the heat in the heat consumed itself
and the air and land grew blacker and blacker.

I once saw a fire move like
coral lightning across the sand
after a meercat maddened
by the cremating arc.

And once, when the heat was like sandpaper, like scorpions,
I saw a salt pan under the high hard sun,
and watched the flamingoes rise, startled,
their underwings protected and pink.

In the veld were thorn trees in patches
like the dregs of other, imaginary gardens,
except in spring, when sticky with yellow life
they had another name, mimosa.

And in the gardens there were always aloes, sharp as blood,
and leathery cannas, all male flowers.
No one has yet put aloes and cannas
into a sweet-smelling basket or pitcher of water.

2

I remember going to a party,
seven and very severe,

in my sober dress two inches over the knee
and my high forehead and my mother's way..
There were lots of children
hiding and seeking, in shifting alliance,
while on the verandah the dog panted
and hopscotch lines simmered on the driveway.
I sat, more sullen than shy, licking my icecream carefully,
hating the aloes and cannas in their tended rows.

Playing games, no one noticed
the air was swelling, heavy on our heads,
and the ground sour with expectation.

Then the storm broke, an exploding rock,
a detonating jewel, its pieces of hot hail
knocking the cannas flat into the earth, puncturing aloes,
and the rain leapt over and over us.

When it was time to go, I ran
across the muddy grass, my back to an imagined breeze,
the yellow ribbons in my hair, loose and lovely,
breaking like waves against my long, thin neck.

Our Sharpeville

I was playing hopscotch on the slate
when miners roared past in lorries,
their arms raised, signals at a crossing,
their chanting foreign and familiar,
like the call and answer of road gangs
across the veld, building hot arteries
from the heart of the Transvaal mine.

I ran to the gate to watch them pass.
And it seemed like a great caravan
moving across the desert to an oasis
I remembered from my Sunday school book:
olive trees, a deep jade pool,
men resting in clusters after a long journey,
the danger of the mission still around them,
and night falling, its silver stars just like the ones
you got for remembering your Bible texts.

Then my grandmother called from behind the front door,
her voice a stiff broom over the steps:
'Come inside; they do things to little girls.'

For it was noon, and there was no jade pool.
Instead, a pool of blood that already had a living name
and grew like a shadow as the day lengthened.
The dead, buried in voices that reached even my gate,
the chanting men on the ambushed trucks,
these were not heroes in my town,
but maulers of children,

doing things that had to remain nameless.
And our Sharpeville was this fearful thing
that might tempt us across the wellswept streets.

If I had turned I would have seen
brocade curtains drawn tightly across sheer net ones,
known there were eyes behind both,
heard the dogs pacing in the locked yard next door.
But, walking backwards, all I felt was shame,
at being a girl, at having been found at the gate,
at having heard my grandmother lie
and at my fear her lie might be true.
Walking backwards, called back,
I returned to the closed rooms, home.

Leavetaking

We are not loving women, having lived long
or intending to. Daughters grow old together.
Sons die, watched over by women.
This isn't Greece but it might as well be.
We move as if robed in black, all widows,
all clean, all careful.

I had one aunt who died young.
They laid her out in white.
She was buried in the late afternoon.
Afterwards I walked back to the house.
My grandmother was waiting,
and the others had prepared food.

This is a dream I have:
I die old but my mourners are older.
They remember my hands and my mother.
My coffin is painted with wild white roses.
There is no keening at all.

At this resort

Tropical plants fringe the sea,
voluptuous branches, heavy with steam and heat
rot onto the moving dunes.
In front of the verandah here
berries swell, red,
crack open like eggs,
their seeds glow poison,
irradiate, glow red.
But for all we know they might have healing properties,
nourish birds, oil flaccid feathers:
they might have saved us.

Really, there is no secret in the view.
I put it there.
No loss at all but landscape, landscape.
The tree bears nothing
that cannot be identified.
The rule of thumb is:
do not eat what even birds avoid.
But here we cannot tell which are the birds.

At the edge of the resort,
beyond the shop, dining room,
bowling greens, the children's trampoline,
the stars dip their wicks
into the waxen fever trees
and shadowy men and boys throat
across the low lagoon.

So lose again a father, lover, son,
to the dark sand

that no one cares to tread upon
unless it is the only pathway
to the rocks and then the hills.

And all along the broken water,
women wardens stand
shaking hands forever at the church door,
greeting the mourners with their dark lapels,
while the coffins heave themselves into the sea.

My father would not show us

Which way do we face to talk to the dead? Rainer Maria Rilke

My father's face
five days dead
is organized for me to see.

It's cold in here
and the borrowed coffin gleams unnaturally;
the pine one has not yet been delivered.

Half-expected this inverted face
but not the soft, for some reason
unfrozen collar of his striped pyjamas.

This is the last time I am allowed
to remember my childhood as it might have been:
a louder, braver place,
crowded, a house with a tin roof
being hailed upon, and voices rising,
my father's wry smile, his half-turned face.

My father would not show us how to die.
He hid, he hid away.
Behind the curtains where his life had been,
the florist's flowers curling into spring,
he lay inside, he lay.

He could recall the rag-and-bone man
passing his mother's gate in the morning light.
Now the tunnelling sound of the dogs next door;
everything he hears is white.

My father could not show us how to die.
He turned, he turned away.
Under the counterpane, without one call
or word or name,
face to the wall, he lay.

2 Where There Is Water

Shadows behind, before

Sky, almond and chalk,
fields bleached with old use,
the highway a silver arrow
through the heart of it all.
If I keep travelling this way
will I know when I've reached the site,
knowledge trickling through my fingers
my hands so full of its soil?

There are two myths of possession here:
the myth of the exile, wanderer,
carrying loss like a bomb under his coat,
a load of winter wood on his back,
mercenary of his own heart's plunder;
and the myth of the householder,
partisan of familiar fields,
who builds his past from mud and water
and his future with the same.

No matter if he visits a valley, the exile
watches from a copse on a windless hill.
But a native in his own place cannot afford
to speculate on the distance to his father's barn.
Each in silence walks a pathway
to a pond that barely moves,
but one turns his back on his own long shadow
and one watches his shadow lead him deep into winter.

In this chill evening ride
the houses buckle into the road's long belt.
Behind a window a woman watches me pass,

matching my eyes as they snatch and drop her.
She sees me, promised unknown distance,
free or urgent to be travelling away;
I see her draw water from a deep metallic well,
I see her candles for the dead.

Two places, two dreams

My child, brought from his own country,
is sleeping in a Cape bed
where the black south-easter
delivers boats and fish
to his hot summer dream
of kelp and tentacles
that hang like fingers from his hands.

In his other dream
pines, like ravens blue with cold,
fly into the ice,
and snow falling from low branches
sifts onto his thin chest.

As he calls in the dark,
'Come', 'Go',
the sea invades the low lagoon
and the red cardinal shaken from his sheet
flies into its dense natal tree.

Old Weather

My son and his father
are walking in the forest
in the cold mist I breathed
to let them know
the land is dangerous.

Vapour moves through them
onto numb branches;
white roots and ledges
are waiting to trip them.

But they play a game
as if it's open country,
shoot arrows into the mist,
find heroes in its shapes,
and their voices are cups
at a picnic, full of bees.

I should follow the walkers
along the bone of land
that juts into the lake's throat.

The mist leaves no spoor,
hasn't a shadow.
My hands rise slowly, like wands.

Skylight

What I want to love
is the empty space
beside my empty body
in the room with skylights
piled with snow
that shudders in the night
as it slips from double-glazed glass,
leaving the stars
balanced on their metal pointes.

Like everyone else I hang desire on stars,
despite everything still think the universe
a coathanger, a Matthew, Mark, Luke and John
bless the bed I lie upon.

Yesterday a junco stunned itself
against a sliding door
so I put it in the sun to die.
Better to die in the glare
than in the dark.
Or so I think so far from home.

In my room high in the pines
no light till nine a.m.
but the sound of snowploughs
churning up winter in the valley below,
making a salt road out of here.

In the rain forest

for Sharron, Canada 1983

There is nothing quieter than this rain
of the high forest at the end of the world.
Where there is too much rain for the huts and the fires
there is only mushroom, moss and the running shadow of the silver doe.

The forest rain is soft and warm
and the heavy wet birds in the leaves are still.
The path is fern again once we have passed
into the dark, the hibernating green.

I remember the rainy season as the season
behind the jacaranda, the season of the sudden purple bruise
on the thighs of the city, afternoon hail
on the hot black tarmac, season of stones.

But this is not the rainy season, this is the rain
that comes out of the tree like wings or air
and into the earth forever; it is the rain that lives,
like a pore, a moon, a ring.

Ruth in the corn

Ontario, 1984

The geese overhead,
the autumn hieroglyph
that everyone can read
and understand.

When you who live and know this place,
when you watch them pass,
you remember their return
even as you lose the sound
of their high migration.

But the others, who see
plantations of olives,
the Southern Cross,
the scrub on the edge of the desert
in the pattern of flight,
when they follow the long geese
overhead, leaving forever,
they want to sing of the south,
even of the southern cities,
even of the small hot rooms.

Sick for home are those watching people
when the fall sky moves its migrating birds.

The two Sherpas

Today, Canadian mountain climber Laurie Skreslet reached the summit of Mount Everest. With him were two Sherpas.

Report by the Canadian Broadcasting Corporation on The National News

Donkeys, clearly, special mountain ones,
or computers to connect The Mountain
with The National.
Or lungs, or esoteric climbing gear,
one for each foot.

Or let's just call them Dan and Sam Sherpa.
Dan didn't need oxygen until the last 200 feet.
Sam had been there twice before.
They might even be good in a crisis,
might even know the way.

Every Canadian deserves one of those Sherpas.
I want one for myself, whatever it is.

Where there is water

for C.C.

I arrived in dark clothes after a long journey. It was still night. I had not been there for many years, and could not recognize the landmarks I once knew well.

1

At my neck a black cameo
mourning's formal clasp
undone by your hand
round my waist your fingers
wild ribbons greeting and leaving
and within
this nacreous love

2

This is when tulip magnolia
exact unflowered
breathes in the growing air
and I moth willow
quiet night
hill over a shadowy city
dream of drawing from a well
a thicket of water

3

I wake to watch
your turning body
face the open door
and the noise
of the unstable city
enters the lightening room

4

I have done this before, going.
You do it well too.
Where there is water, or in sight of the sea,
gypsies gather.

Woman, leaning away

He hands it to me
as if it were her wedding ring
the picture of his mother
remoter than the island
she couldn't leave.

She is leaning away from herself,
from the photograph, from us,
towards something out there,
a tree or stone or colour.
Her dress is soft, unstylish,
and perhaps her hands are folded.
He will give her anything,
corals, pearls, all his photographs of her
if she will turn just once
to see him watching her
the way one watches for a bird
whose sound in the dense green
promises shape just before it is silent again.

I think of her as a woman
whose eyes must have been grey
who said nothing of her own mother
or the things she heard as a child
on a balcony over the narrow streets
leaning towards the sea.

When her children left for the mainland
she may have laid out her clothes on the bed,
opened the shutters to air the empty rooms,
then turned to stand,

stiller than the photograph,
near a trellis of sweet smells
so thick it concealed the hills.

Only afterwards
lying beside him in the cool
I realize this was a test
to see if I too would lean
away from him and the open window
while I looked on the photograph
of his silent mother.

Dolphin Eater

There was nothing else to eat.
So I ate the dolphin
and asked my friend
never ever to tell.

Like lightning
that night
sea struck me
and I screamed in my sleep
for a boat to take me back
to the first shore
where I had eaten no dolphin.

In my eyes dolphins dancing
in the bay close to shore
a gift of the evening tide
to the strollers on the beach.
In my mouth, dolphin.

I tricked the silent ferryman,
gave beads for land,
and the silver cargo of the dhow
discharged into my palm.

Nothing will save me now
in the waves off the cliffs.
I will not be brought home
on the leeside of a dolphin's fin.

Enduring your devil

In the cottage the candles flickered for sanity.
You say you were alone except for
wind off the cliffs and the devil.

You could not shut the door
that swung wide into that place.
Even the crucifix could not do that.

You ask me to remember
the blasted heath, the slouching beast,
the Florence of Savanarola.

But I hear only your thin words:
'I stayed awake all night
watching the open door, keeping the evil out.'

It's no use looking for comfort in the Apocrypha,
in the images you subpoena
at the crossroads where suicides are buried.

You cannot survive this devil
with an arsenal of texts and spells.
You cannot keep him out with a guard at the gate.

Blow out the candles,
Let the cliff winds blow.
Poor windswept devil, take him in,
Get to know him well.

Dream of a trophy

In my dream you are a mendicant
carrying an onyx bowl.
I feed you violets and small roasted rats
and you sing for your sorrows
and eat out of my hand.

The weight of your cape is the weight of this dream
and is tied to your neck by an emerald clasp.
But your body beneath is battered and thin
like a sliver of glass or of ice.

I polish the dents in your dream body
and see myself there, polishing.
Your collarbone gleams like pewter.
I could hang your cheeks on the wall, like plates.
You are what I want you to be, at night.

Woman in the glass

I am not the woman in the train
who pulls your hand between her legs
and then looks out of the window.

I am not the woman with the henna hair
in a city street, who never says a word
but beckons you, beckons you.

Nor am I the woman in the glass
who looks at you look at her
and the glass smokes over.

Nor the woman who holds you
whilst you call out the names of lost lovers
as you will call out this one.

Nor am I the woman in the dark
whose silence is the meteor
in the sky of your conversation.

That woman:
bent over, offering her sex to you
like a globe of garlic, asking for nothing;
the one without fingerprints,
hiding in the amulet of your protection;
the one surrounded by photographers
printing her supple smile, her skin:
that woman.

I stand to the side and watch her,

widow-virgin, burn on your pyre.
Acrobat falling into a net of ash,
in the flames her mouth drips wax,
her eyebrows peel off,
her sex unstitches its tiny mirrors.

Your woman: cousin, sister, twin.
You want her burning, distant, dumb.
I want to save, and tear, her tongue.

To a would-be lover

I once knew a man who made love
with pockets of iron filings.
The machines were oiled, the pistons shone,
we were stapled together and sent through a shute.

And you would probably balance
like a gymnast on the cross-bar,
just before the triple turn,
with the air still, the audience still,
energy parallel with intention.

I cannot love athletes or makers of metal things
or anyone associated with Concorde.
I like the sillier body, earthbound,
with its many joints and dents:
a squat figure on a sweaty mat.
The delicious fiction, love,
must dangle its infinitives,
forget to ciose its clauses,
offer alternative endings,
a hero whose shirt hangs out
and a heroine who trips over the bed
because her contacts are lost under the sink.

Praise be the inelegance of ordinary love
when the children on the street
are skidding on skateboards
and the doorbell rings and has to be ignored
when the pillows are too soft
and the feet are much too cold.

So, pyrotechnic suitor,
your skin is far too sleek,
your arms too architectural,
your timing much too neat.
I'm sure you'll find another
to watch you in the mirror
but I must refuse your offer
and decline to conjugate.

Words of love

1

He said:
'Are you happy?'
'Are you alright?'
'What are you thinking?'
'Are you alright?'
He said: 'These words,
the fetishes of early anxious love.'

She said:
'How strange and how familiar
the breathing of a new lover.'
'Are you alright?'
'Are you still there?'
She said: 'The mist at this time of year
confuses everything.'

2

Oh how we swallow, how then we carry
in our pouches the words of our lovers
as if they are our own.
Our mouths are icing tubes and vases
and we lipstick the words of love
onto hall mirrors, onto ourselves,
or have them implanted
silicon deep in our pointed breasts.

Knowing the thoughts of the beloved,
having the same thoughts,
or something close enough, like false teeth,
caps, crowns, bridges,

letting them rise out of our mouths
into bubbles, into an adult comic strip:
this is called *love*.

Till the bubbles blow off the page,
are spiked on thorntrees,
collapse like Chinese lanterns,
or we chew them like gum,
the words of our lovers,
gag, spit out at last
a trickle of sounds
more like our own:
this is called *betrayal*.

3

No woman ever says
'It's in the pipeline'
even in countries with large oil reserves
and women on the rigs.

Visitor

When you turn to me, carrying your weight on your side
like a gypsy with a pail, I must stroke you cleverly,
gently, taking care to be silent: sounds carry.

You are a guest here, and your pain is unfamiliar to me
even when you turn like this into my hospitable hands
and I have to call you my own.

On a still afternoon, you visit your request on me
that I cannot answer, cannot refuse.
You are thinner than I remember.

Arrangement: a poem for myself

In the room with a round mahogany table
I recognize myself, arranging the flowers.
From spring somewhere else I bring
freesias, anemone, yellow roses
and jasmine, fragrant as water.
There is only one rule:
from all sides the arrangement must look perfect.
It must not prefer the window seat
or the large oil painting
or even myself, who appears to be judging.

But freesias are so light
they want to fly like butterflies above the other flowers.
I let them rise and settle
while the roses drink and drink,
water entering them like blood.
One jasmine blossom is so Japanese
it belongs in a vase by itself
in another room, with mirrors.
Stems must be cut to size.
Anything brown has to go.
Even one shooting star
that scatters its petals like ore
on the round mahogany table
must be gathered into newspaper
and carried from the room.

This culling of flowers like young impala
they say is 'for the sake of the whole',
but what I mean is that
I have to choose flowers

that will live in this vase
as if it is the earth
and the death of flowers
that cannot transform themselves,
even when my hands are full of their sacrifice,
is like air in my lungs.

This thing we learn from others

From the hitchhiker whose head
falls against your shoulder in his sleep
as you swerve in the dark rain,
from two small boys waving
at a Safari Tour bus,
from others, that stowaway for instance,
who gave himself up because
from his hiding place
he couldn't smell the sea,
and from people who bury their dogs
in gardens, at night,
remembering the date until they are old.

They say if your mother held you
on her right side, head in the moist curve
of her arm, you are lonely,
and if she held you on her left,
her breast breathing into your ear,
you are lonely.

To be thus
is what we should have expected.

Only, at neap tide,
its moon just a glance
over the wet uncovered miles of sand,
the rocks white and black mica in the dark,
and waves which had buried themselves
at our feet, now trebling quietly
far out there

made us come close
to the fire on the beach,
made us think it possible
to stay that way,
scooping warm coals into the heart.

3 Small Passing

Women, mourning

In memory of Anita Lindenberg

We enter the doorway on dark stone
and pass calligraphic paintings and toys,
piles of winter fruit, and knitting
that hangs from a chair like a weaver bird's nest,
to find our way to the walled garden.

Around her, an apron of daughters tie a loose bow.
The smallest tugs at her life as if it's a nipple,
recites sunny rhymes and wants to be sung to.
The eldest speaks of leaving but stays among them
wearing hoops in her ears and her mother's rings.
The middle two swim in currents around her,
their fins brushing her sides,
and sometimes they surface to gulp in her air.
When her sister arrives, they touch fingers,
netting their girlhood
in the cat's cradle they laced long ago.

And the movement among these women
is a mnemonic that makes us long for forgetfulness,
for a plain where the only current
is a thin wisp of cloud over its shadow.
For they are weaving reeds beside a hut and an impossible mountain,
baskets holding earth and water,
and we know they will make a gift of their work
to us, to bear on our heads,
the careful visitors who stepped into the circle
hoping it would be a charm.

For our friend is dying.
Death grows inside her
and there is no nursery song
soft enough to kill it.
Her face is scaffolding, her eyes too bright.
But her arms are so full of hands
when you come to her door
all you feel are her hands.

And this is what we cannot ask:
at night in the pool of her daughters' breathing,
does she lie awake,
widely awake,
holding her own hands,
to keep them from rising,
to keep them from her face?

On her way home

For Mary Anne

This is her favourite view on her way home:
when the road leans suddenly
towards a grey outcrop of rock and shadow,
a hill pockmarked by aloes,
when the sky is dead clear, the sun dead centre,
and the others driving past
turn to their conversations
about resorts along the river further on.

She stopped once to walk in the place.
Her children ran ahead, looking for snakes,
feeling the heat fill their shoes
like thick dust, imagining leopards and vultures
and the weapons they would use to subdue them.
The sun settled, a horsefly on her head:
she would not brush it away.

Far away on a black flank she saw the children,
grey goats on another continent,
heard from over the hill the stuck sound
of cars immobile in liquefied tar,
bent to see the order of large red ants on the sand,
felt their filings on her bare legs.

Heat bearing down
on her neck, behind her knees.
In her head sun stroking her,
clay beads of sweat in her head,

in her pupils blacker and blacker.
The skull of a sheep made her think
of erecting gazebos in the place
and she laughed out loud
so far from the river
remembering the futile shade of willows.

When the boys came upon her
looking straight into the sun,
they were large white rings in her viewing.
Their hands burning, they dozed fitfully
the half hour home, not noticing
how she stopped singing
when the road entered their valley
shining with the ribbons of irrigated colour.

Road through Lesotho

From over the corrugated hills we are sighted
driving along the inhospitable road, casting a lumpy shadow.
His arms flapping, mouth shuttering,
the boy who cares for his father's cattle
hurdles towards us, a missile of expectations.

We keep on moving. Will he reach us before we swerve
beyond, into a village of women and children?
The clouds muscle. Thunder and electric light.
No time to stop, play Lady Bountiful.

But there he is before us, blocking escape,
a toll gate into Africa.
His breath grinds dry and hard.
He has three clay oxen for sale.
'Ten cents missus, ten cents missus?'

Am I a Ten Cents Missus? I do not know his name.
He bends his knees of warring bones.
His hands are curved and small.
I am a visitor with things in my pockets.
It is shameful to give trifles to children.

But unsmilingly he claims his payment,
not caring for my guidebook scruples.
Herder of cattle, other plans in his head,
he has been on the hills all day, waiting for us.

found poem 1

The toilets are
being left
in an unhygienic state
by the people
who use them.
There is a group
among them
that want to
overthrow all order.

Buckets are
being overturned.

Who these militants are
I don't know.
In any case
it isn't me.

(Mr Rust, Town Clerk, Victoria West.
Cape Times, 25 July 1985.)

found poem 2

'I realized here is trouble
and immediately gave the order to fire.
I aimed at the leader
but he disappeared from my vision.
He had been shot
by somebody else.'

(Lt. Fouche, reported in *Cape Times* Saturday, 30 March 1985.)

Stones, Sky, Radio

Around the roots of the tree
the children are dicing with stones.
The sky is immense as the sky,
the sun is as hot as the noonday sun,
the red ants are industrious as ants.
The children are dicing with stones.

Across the grey veld a man is walking.
He is neither young nor old.
He is holding a stick and kicking a tin
and walks like a man walking
across the veld in the dust.

In the distance a radio crackles
out of a cluster of huts.
This is not a sign of life.
It is a radio in the village.

There is nothing else to see or hear
at this time and place, apparently.
The children are still dicing with stones.

Al wat kind is

They took all that was child in the house.
Resident of Victoria West, reporting on police action in the town.

They took all that was child
and in the dark closed room
visions of a ripe split melon
were at the tip of a knife
they held to the child's dry tongue.

All that was child
lies on the tarmac;
the intestines spill
like beans from a sack,
seaweed from the winter sea.

The bird of state has talons
and shit that drops like lead.
Its metal wings corrode the streets,
it hatches pools of blood.

A stone against a tank is a stone against a tank
but a bullet in a child's chest rips into the heart of the house.

But when in time the single stones
compact their weight and speed together,
roll up the incline towards the lamvanger's lair,
crushing sand into rock, rock into boulder,
boulder into mountain, mountain into sky,
then the lungs of the bird will choke,
the wings will blister and crack,
at last the eyes will glaze, defeated.

And this torn light,
this long torn light
will repair itself
out of the filaments of children,
and all that is child will return to the house,
will open the doors of the house.

Small Passing

For a woman whose baby died stillborn, and who was told by a man to stop mourning, 'because the trials and horrors suffered daily by black women in this country are more significant than the loss of one white child'.

1

In this country you may not
suffer the death of your stillborn,
remember the last push into shadow and silence,
the useless wires and cords on your stomach,
the nurse's face, the walls, the afterbirth in a basin.
Do not touch your breasts
still full of purpose.
Do not circle the house,
pack, unpack the small clothes.
Do not lie awake at night hearing
the doctor say 'It was just as well'
and 'You can have another.'
In this country you may not
mourn small passings.

See: the newspaper boy in the rain
will sleep tonight in a doorway.
The woman in the busline
may next month be on a train
to a place not her own.
The baby in the backyard now
will be sent to a tired aunt,
grow chubby, then lean,
return a stranger.
Mandela's daughter tried to find her father
through the glass. She thought they'd let her touch him.

And this woman's hands are so heavy when she dusts
the photographs of other children
they fall to the floor and break.
Clumsy woman, she moves so slowly
as if in a funeral rite.

On the pavements the nannies meet.
These are legal gatherings.
They talk about everything, about home,
while the children play among them,
their skins like litmus, their bonnets clean.

2

Small wrist in the grave.
Baby no one carried live
between houses, among trees.
Child shot running,
stones in his pocket,
boy's swollen stomach
full of hungry air.
Girls carrying babies
not much smaller than themselves.
Erosion. Soil washed down to the sea.

3

I think these mothers dream
headstones of the unborn.
Their mourning rises like a wall
no vine will cling to.
They will not tell you your suffering is white.
They will not say it is just as well.
They will not compete for the ashes of infants.
I think they may say to you:

Come with us to the place of mothers.
We will stroke your flat empty belly,
let you weep with us in the dark,
and arm you with one of our babies
to carry home on your back.

Come with us to the place of marbles.
We will strike your flat empty bell.
let you weep with us in the dark,
and [illegible] without [illegible] our babies
to carve name on your neck.

Faint Remains of Existence

Lucinda Carey

Indigo Dreams Publishing

First Edition: Faint Remains of Existence
First published in Great Britain in 2013 by:
Indigo Dreams Publishing
24, Forest Houses
Cookworthy Moor
Halwill
Beaworthy
Devon
EX21 5UU

www.indigodreams.co.uk

ISBN 978-1-909357-33-4

British Library Cataloguing in Publication Data. A CIP record for this book can be obtained from the British Library.

Designed and typeset in Palatino Linotype by Indigo Dreams.

Cover image by Lucinda Carey.
Cover design by Ronnie Goodyer.

Printed and bound in Great Britain by Imprint Academic, Exeter.

Papers used by Indigo Dreams are recyclable products made from wood grown in sustainable forests following the guidance of the Forest Stewardship Council.